February 24, 2018

Dear Dale,

My heart is filled with joy and gratitude for the beautiful gift of knowledge and understanding you have shared with me this week. Your sweet spirit has touched my heart and your gentle words that have opened God's Word in new ways have inspired me and blessed me beyond words! Thank you! I pray that this little story from my heart will bless you with joy and hope as we anticipate the great reunion.

Love and Blessings,
Rita Brown
Colossians 3:1-2
2 Corinthians 4:16-18

My First Day in Heaven

My First Day in Heaven

Rita Brown

LEAFWOOD
P U B L I S H E R S
an imprint of Abilene Christian University Press

MY FIRST DAY IN HEAVEN

an imprint of Abilene Christian University Press

ISBN 978-0-89112-394-1
LCCN 2015005566

Printed in Canada

SONG CREDITS:
"Holy, Holy, Holy." John Dykes and Reginald Heber. Public Domain.
"Amazing Grace." John Newton and John Rees. Public Domain.
"I've Read the Back of the Book." Roger Bennett. Used by permission.

LIBRARY OF CONGRESS CATALOGING-IN-PUBLICATION DATA
Brown, Rita, 1946-
  My first day in heaven / Rita Brown.
     pages cm
  ISBN 978-0-89112-394-1
  1. Heaven--Fiction. I. Title.
  PS3602.R722695M93 2015
  813'.6--dc23

2015005566

Leafwood Publishers is an imprint of Abilene Christian University Press
ACU Box 29138
Abilene, Texas 79699
1-877-816-4455
www.leafwoodpublishers.com

15 16 17 18 19 20 / 7 6 5 4 3 2 1

To my husband, Dale, my constant encourager,
my six wonderful children,
my beautiful daughters-in-law
and sons-in-law,
and all my precious grandchildren.

Be there!

And to my mother and father,
who showed me the way
and are there waiting for me now.

And to Connor,
the first of our kids and grandkids to get home.
His thirteen wonderful years on this earth continue
to inspire me and many others to want to "be there."
See you at the house, Connor.

And above all,
to Him who is the true Author
of this happy story.

Acknowledgments

*M*y deep, heartfelt thanks to my sweet friend, Connie Tate, who never stopped encouraging me to publish this story.

And my sincere gratitude to Ann Adams and Tom Reed whose encouragement and expertise made this book come together.

And to my precious Bible Study girls—Pam, Celeste, Patty, and D'Nese—who walked beside me, providing everything from just the right word when I needed it to constant cheers of support.

And to the wonderful Mary Hollingsworth whose wisdom, experience, and gracious reassurance gave new life to it.

And to so many others whose never-ending encouragement through the years has kept this book going.

This is a fictional story. Although this story is derived from Scripture, it is not intended to be a theologically precise representation of heaven, but rather the author's impression of how it could be.

Preface

It was a beautiful, crisp, autumn afternoon, and I was sitting in the big blue chair in our den reading a biblical passage that just happened to be about heaven. I have always encouraged my children and others to use their imaginations when reading Scripture in order to make the reality of God's Word come alive. I closed my eyes, leaned my head back, and began to ponder what heaven would really be like.

Thoughts, pictures, and scriptures began to tumble through my mind. I grabbed the nearest scrap of paper and began jotting down ideas. Later, as I went about my work, more ideas of what heaven might be like kept popping into my head. I continued to grab more scraps and jot down more ideas. (I have learned as I grow older that thoughts seldom pass through more than once, and if I don't write them down immediately, they may be lost forever.)

By the end of the day, I had been thoroughly energized by my thoughts of heaven and had gathered quite a handful of little pieces of paper with scribbled reflections. I carefully saved all my little scraps of notes, thinking that someday it would be fun to write a story about heaven.

Many months later I was asked to teach the first class of the new year for our church ladies' class. The year just ending had been a busy, stressful, and somewhat discouraging year, and I was feeling drained and uninspired. The whole world seemed quite depressing to me at that moment.

"Lord, what word of encouragement for a new year could I possibly have for these ladies?"

All of a sudden I remembered the scraps of paper and began to search diligently for them. I finally found them, still just scribbled random thoughts going in every direction on bits of paper. I sat down at the computer with my scraps and my Bible and began to type. It was so much fun to whisk myself away into the very presence of God, where all the problems, disappointments, and stresses were replaced with a vision of hope and joy. Once again I found myself energized as my emotions moved from tears

to laughter and back again. When I typed the final period, I felt God had given me the encouraging words I needed to share, words which reminded me once again that the struggles, disappointments, failures, and pain we face daily on this earth are not the end of the Story.

In the years since I read this story to that group of ladies, it has been shared with many others in various ways. I am always amazed at the enthusiastic response. We live in a world that is decaying day by day in every way, and suffering is universal. It seems that all of us get caught up in our personal situations and easily lose touch with the end of the Story that can give us direction, encouragement, and hope. People everywhere seem to yearn for the encouragement from God's promise of the glorious outcome He has planned for His people. When our oldest son was a young teenager, he came in one day and shared with me the words to a song he had just heard on the radio: "We win, we win, hallelujah, we win; I read the back of the book, and we win!" There is much strength to be gained from peeking ahead to the end of the Story, realizing that it will be worth everything.

My prayer is that you, no matter what your present struggles and disappointments, will gain renewed hope and encouragement by catching a glimpse of the incredible future God is preparing for you. For those of you who may be dealing with the death of a loved one, my deepest, heartfelt prayer is that you may be blessed with special peace and comfort from God's promises. For all of us, I pray that God can use these limited human words to inspire and motivate us to seek to know God more fully and to live our daily lives totally for Him in anticipation of that moment when we will see His loving face, and He will say to each of His own, *"Enter in, good and faithful servant."*

For our light and momentary troubles

are achieving for us an eternal glory

that far outweighs them all.

—2 Corinthians 4:17

Then each of them was given a white robe.

—Revelation 6:11

I do not remember many details of the end of my journey, except that it was such a relief when I was finally able to close my eyes. The next thing I knew, I opened my eyes to see a silver-haired, gentle-looking man dressed in brilliant white standing beside my bed.

"Let's go, Jenny! Your limo awaits!" he said gently.

My *what?* Where was I anyway? For some reason I glanced down at my hands. Where were my wrinkles and my age spots?

Before I could ponder the possibilities, the kind stranger reached for my hand. "Here," he said, "let me help you with your new robe."

"My new robe?" I replied weakly.

A strange peace and strong sense of well-being began to envelop me. His tender eyes met mine as he held out the most beautiful full-length white garment I had ever beheld. The outside was soft, white velvet trimmed in delicate, handmade lace embroidered with tiny pearls.

The lining was of the purest white satin. As I slipped it on and felt the luxuriously smooth satin caressing my skin, I began to feel very special. He slipped perfectly matched slippers onto my feet and then motioned for me to look into a full-length mirror in the corner of the room.

Hesitating, I asked in a trembling voice, "Who are you? Is this a dream? Am I real? Are you real?" The questions came tumbling out.

"Oh, I assure you," he laughed softly, "that *you* are real, *I* am real, and *this* is no dream. I have been sent to help you get ready and to escort you!"

"Escort me? Where am I going?"

Suddenly the reality of the situation began to settle in my soul. That strange peace and sense of well-being snuggled around my heart. Without any sense of fear, but with a rising joyful anticipation, I looked into the eyes of the stranger, knowing assuredly that something wonderful was unfolding. Once again, I looked down at my now beautiful hands—new hands—and walked slowly to the mirror. My new robe swished elegantly in the silence of my ears. I slowly raised my eyes and gasped as I gazed at the new person staring back at me from the mirror. My

mind tumbled with disconnected phrases: *But we shall all be changed . . . [He] will transform our lowly bodies . . . each of them was given a white robe . . .* I stroked the sleeve of the soft velvet robe as I worked to pull distant thoughts from my memory—dim thoughts that were now suddenly quite relevant. The stranger peered over my shoulder into the mirror with an amused look on his face as he noted my mixture of confusion and exhilaration.

"Does it fit?" he asked, somewhat playfully.

"Oh yes," I whispered, "as if it had been made just for me."

The amused look became a twinkling smile. "I have one more thing," he mused as he turned to an elegant, round box covered with white silk interwoven with fragile strands of gold threads.

As I watched in the mirror, he carefully removed the lid of the box and lovingly lifted out an exquisite gold crown gloriously sparkling with emeralds, pearls, amethysts, and other jewels, each extravagantly highlighted with brilliant diamonds. I whirled around from the image in the mirror and stood absolutely speechless and motionless as I beheld the splendor of the object the stranger was now extending toward me. I was totally mesmerized by the flawless simplicity and perfect elegance of the headpiece while my mind wrestled with a truth that I was not quite ready to accept.

More distant phrases nudged my thoughts: *Will receive the crown . . . that God has promised . . . the crown of glory that will never fade away . . .* My complete paralysis was finally relieved by a single tear sliding slowly down my cheek.

"Come, come, child, you're not going to need those tears anymore. Are you ready to try it on? It's yours, you know."

"*Mine?* Are you sure?" My mind was refusing to acknowledge that I was here, much less participating in this awesome scenario.

"Watch in the mirror now," he said. "I'm sure it will just fit."

I turned silently toward the mirror and watched breathlessly as he placed the magnificent crown atop my head. He was right! It fit perfectly. My eyes gazed in wide-eyed wonder as the reflection from each jewel glittered and danced.

Amazingly the crown felt as light on my head as the aluminum foil crowns I had fashioned in Bible class as a little girl. Scenes of chubby fingers covered with glue and glitter, carefully donning a newly created "crown of righteousness," drifted across my mind with a newly acquired understanding. I checked my fingers for signs of glitter, but instead found myself peering once again at those brand new hands. I had carefully refrained from touching the crown in an attempt to avoid bringing this wonderful happening to a premature close, but now I slowly raised my fingers to lightly brush the twinkling jewels.

"Oh!" I cried, as it tilted slightly at my touch. "I think I ought to put it back in its box. It, uh . . . it doesn't feel quite right yet. May I?" I asked looking uncertainly at the stranger.

"Certainly, child. It's yours to do with as you wish," he replied tenderly as he gently lifted the crown from my head and returned it to the silken box. Replacing the lid, he laid the box in my arms. "Come now; let's get on to the limousine. You have a big day ahead."

Before I could react, I was staring into the gleaming interior of a long, glistening, white limousine. The stranger was holding the door and motioning for me to enter. I eased into the spacious area, sinking into the luxuriously soft lambskin leather seat. Everything was designed for regal comfort and thorough pampering. I snuggled down into my robe, draping it with care around my ankles. I clutched the silken round box in my lap. The stranger slid in beside me just in time as the Cinderella coach glided away. We were surrounded by a tranquil mist as the hushed music of harps drifted around us.

"How are you doing so far?" the stranger queried thoughtfully.

"Uh . . . great! I think." Once again the overwhelming sense of peace and well-being prompted a lazy smile across my face. I suppressed a little girl urge to ask, "How long until we get there?"

Besides, time and reality were somehow blending into an undefined form like the mist that surrounded us.

Since we are surrounded by

such a great cloud of witnesses

. . . let us run with perseverance

the race marked out for us.

—Hebrews 12:1

*S*uddenly ahead, a bright light cut through the mist—brighter than anything I could relate to from my remembered past. We were approaching something magnificent—a structure that went beyond my ability to imagine or describe. I chuckled aloud as the memory of a long-ago, teenage son quipping, "Awesome, Mom!" popped into my head. At my audible chuckle, the stranger gave me a puzzled look. "Awesome," I said softly. He grinned with understanding.

My sense of excitement was mounting as the vast, square structure loomed ever larger. It was much more expansive than my eyes could take in. Its multilayered foundation glistened with jewels of every color. From the direction we were approaching, there seemed to be three gates. As we drew close the gates appeared to be three enormous pearls, gleaming iridescent in the bright light. A loud noise began to vibrate my senses. It was the sound of shouting, growing more and more distinct as we turned toward the middle gate.

At that moment one of the gigantic pearl gates swung open on its massive gold filigree hinges, and the sound of shouting became a deafening roar. Straight ahead, just beyond the gate, stretched a seemingly interminable shining, golden roadway lined on each side with droves of people, all shouting and waving as our limousine entered.

"What is all this commotion about?" I asked the stranger at the top of my voice so as to be heard above the din of the crowds around us. "It looks like a parade for a war hero or something." I was stretching my neck trying to get a glimpse of whom or what all this uproar was about.

I noticed that the stranger was watching me with a look of merriment in his eyes. Determined not to miss out if someone famous was passing by, I ignored his apparently private joke and continued searching out the windows for a clue to this madness. The sense of peace that I had been enjoying in the quiet serenity of the limousine ride was being replaced by a sense of uneasiness and confusion. As I peered out the window on my side, it

seemed almost as if all these people were shouting and waving at *me.*

All at once, amid the pandemonium, I thought I heard my name. "Jenny! Jenny!" I could not believe my ears. "Jenny! Jenny!"

Now it was so clear. These people were all shouting my name! They were cheering and waving at me as though I was the winner of a marathon race, and they were rooting me across the finish line. As understanding was jolting my consciousness, my senses were exploding with volatile emotions. The crowd blurred through my eyes, now swimming in tears. My heart seemed to be racing to catch up with what was happening inside and all around me. I caught one momentary glimpse of the delighted stranger watching me with pride and satisfaction before turning back to the crowd.

I was battling emotions and tears to bring everything into focus when suddenly one face stood out among all the others with startling clarity. A sob of recognition caught in my throat as my eyes looked squarely into the eyes of my daddy. There he was, cheering once again for his little girl.

As the limo passed slowly by, I could read his lips saying, "I've been waiting for you, little one." I could see my mother standing beside my daddy, her eyes brimming with tears of happiness, staring with wide-eyed wonder. Beside him I found my brother, Rob, waving uncontrollably and hollering at the top of his lungs in his normal exuberant style, "You made it, little sister, you made it!" There was Granny, too, smiling with peaceful satisfaction.

As the limousine rounded a curve in the road, I gasped as I saw a young man with dark brown hair and freckles sprinkled across his nose waving frantically. "Grandma, Grandma," he shouted. It was Connor!

Oh, how sweet those words sounded to my ears. Oh, how I had longed for this day. For the very last time my mind went back to the scene of the accident on that lonely highway where I had knelt beside the broken body of my precious grandson—the scene that had played in my mind over and over through the years as the tears flowed freely. The thought of this reunion had been my hope— had been the only comfort for the anguish of my broken heart. Now, as his sweet smile and exuberant voice filled

my heart with joy once again, I was overwhelmed with gratitude. All those things I had said and thought about seeing Connor again one day were true! *It was all true!*

"Please, please," I pleaded with the stranger. "Can we stop for just one hug?"

He smiled gently and assured me that there would be plenty of time for an eternity of hugs and visiting, but for now there were even better things ahead. I strained my neck to catch one more glimpse of Connor as we continued my victory parade.

Other faces from long ago began to emerge from the crowd. The parade of cheering witnesses went on and on. I had always wondered what it would be like to come home after winning several gold medals at the Olympics or hitting the winning home run in the final game of the World Series. I supposed that it would not even compare to what was happening to me at this very moment. I had the overwhelming feeling that these people were proud of me—very proud; that I—ordinary, plain, unexceptional, everyday Jenny—was a winner! What an experience!

In my Father's house are

many rooms. . . . I am going

there to prepare

a place for you. . . .

I will come back and take you

to be with me that you also may

be where I am.

—John 14:2–3

The crowd finally began to thin out as we approached a deep, circular driveway ahead. I sank back into the seat and closed my eyes to relive what had just taken place. I wanted to grasp the feelings to my bosom and savor them slowly and selectively again and again. Just as I was mentally pulling out the first recollection, the stranger interrupted my thoughts. "You may want to open your eyes for what is up ahead," he almost whispered.

I was not quite ready to let go of the incident I had just experienced, so I almost decided to pretend that I hadn't heard him.

"This is always one of my favorite views," he murmured.

Somewhat reluctantly, but still finding my curiosity quite intact on this most unusual day, I slowly opened one eye. Immediately I opened both eyes very wide and jolted up in my seat to get a better view.

There, straight ahead down a long, glittering, golden driveway lined with huge trees, stood a massive, majestic mansion. The huge trees, laden with colorful fruit, were draped over the driveway. Unending expanses of perfectly manicured lawns stretched in every direction.

As we neared the front of the mansion, the most noticeable architectural feature was an immense, shimmering, gold fountain with solid-gold cherubim lifting an elegant gold bowl. Crystal clear water gurgled down to an even larger gold bowl with a rim displaying thousands of perfectly formed gold roses.

I had to giggle when I saw the fountain. I remembered how many times my husband, Dan, had told me that we could not have a fountain, even though I really wanted one, because there was just no way to keep one clean with West Texas sand blowing so much of the time.

"I guess they don't have much West Texas sand here, huh?" I murmured half to myself.

In mock seriousness the stranger replied, "Oh no, ma'am. We passed the Texas border sometime back."

The front of the mansion was dominated by an extensive front porch with its roof supported by enormous carved, gold pillars reaching several stories in height. Wide steps of white marble descended to a walkway of white marble stones set together with gold mortar. On each side of the walkway, white marble planters with brilliant gold carvings on the sides held pink and red roses in full, perfect bloom.

The scene was breathtaking. I could not keep from noticing that there was no sign of decay or wear of any kind—no tarnish, no dirt, no weeds; everything was immaculate. Perhaps, though, the highlight for me was the pristine, white, wooden rocking chairs complete with white velvet cushions that were beckoning from the front porch. Someone had thought of everything.

As our limo was pulling up in front, my attention was drawn to the towering front doors made of carved gold with leaded crystal panels inset in the gold. Just then the massive front door opened, and a man dressed in brilliant, blinding white crossed the front porch and descended the steps quickly. In a flash He had reached the limousine and was opening the door.

I found myself gazing into the most tender, understanding eyes I had ever seen, being drawn into the very

depths of this man with instant recognition. Immediately my body and my entire being felt calm and peaceful with total release.

Looking deeply into my eyes, He whispered softly, "Jenny."

My heart melted at the sound of *my* name on *His* lips. I fell into the arms of my Jesus. I was *home.*

He held me tenderly until I truly felt as if I were floating. Finally He lifted my chin, looked deeply into my eyes, and said simply, "Welcome home."

He took my arm gently, and we began to ascend the steps together. I turned with belated awareness to say good-bye and to thank the kind stranger, but there was no sign of him or the limousine—only the lingering warmth of his kindness. I turned my full attention to Jesus as I gathered my robe to keep from tripping, trying not to drop my precious crown, which was still in its box.

"I have your room all ready for you," Jesus said eagerly. "I think it will be just right for you. Here, let me help you with that box. I know you are ready for a rest."

I just could not take my eyes off Him. It was actually *Him.* The words that kept running through my head

were familiar: *Do not let your hearts be troubled. Trust in God, trust also in Me. In my Father's house are many rooms . . . I am going there to prepare a place for you . . . I will come back and take you to be with me that you also may be where I am.*

How many times had I turned to those words for comfort and assurance, but now it was really happening. I was actually ascending the steps of the mansion that I had always dreamed of, *and Jesus was escorting me.* This was no longer faith; it was *reality.*

I could not wait to see the room that Jesus had prepared just for me. A thousand questions began to emerge from my trancelike state. I had often daydreamed of being able to ask Jesus anything I wanted. Now, crazy as it might seem, the most urgent question tickling my curiosity was not some deep, theological, puzzling question; I simply wondered what color my new room was. I was not sure whether it was comforting or frightening to know I was still me, even in *heaven.*

Jesus turned to me with a broad smile on His face. "I'm sure you are going to like it. Trust me."

I returned His smile with total confidence that He would surely know what I needed for eternity better than I would. We now stepped into a broad entry, gorgeous and grand in every exquisite detail. Passing down a long, elegant hall, we ascended a wide staircase carpeted with plush, velvety white carpet.

As we passed down the next hall, Jesus looked down at me with a twinkle in His eye.

"*Bright orange* is your favorite color, isn't it?" He laughed gently at the startled look on my face. "Remember, I have promised you *rest* in this place," He said with a chuckle.

He stopped at a large, white door beautifully carved with roses and tiny birds. Turning the gold doorknob, He quietly ushered me into a spacious, luxurious room. My eyes were taking in every incredible detail of this quietly tranquil, elegant room done in shades of soft, azure blue and ivory. He had obviously prepared every last detail exactly to my liking. He knew it was perfect, and so did I.

"Thank you," I whispered, and His look of total understanding told me that I did not need to say another word.

"Now, dear Jenny," He said lightly, "we have some business to attend to. We have an appointment with Father a little later, but first I want you to get some long-awaited rest. I shall return when you are rested, and we will visit for a little while before we keep our appointment."

"Uh . . . what time do I need to be ready?"

"Time?" He chuckled. "You just rest, and it will all happen just as it has been planned from the beginning. There is no more time, Jenny. It will all happen with perfect timing."

I could tell that there were a few things I was going to have to adjust to, but right now it really did not seem important. Somehow the fear and anxiety that would have seemed appropriate in view of the coming events were only vague concepts in my memory of long ago. *Now* was wonderful. *Now* I was going to lie on that downy soft bed and sink into those satin sheets and rest. Happiness and peace embraced every fiber of my being.

"I will be back, Jenny," Jesus whispered softly.

I remember carefully hanging my robe on a satin hanger and donning a pale-pink, silk gown before

snuggling down into the most comfortable place I had ever been. Feelings of pure perfection caressed my spirit. My crown lay nestled in the white, silken box on the table beside my bed.

Blessed is the man who

perseveres under trial,

because when he has stood the

test, he will receive the

crown of life

that God has promised

to those who love him.

—James 1:12

$\mathcal{T}$he next thing I knew, there was a soft knock on the door. I was totally rested and eager for *now*. I slipped into my white robe and greeted Jesus with enthusiasm. He smiled into my eyes and motioned me to a pair of crystal doors leading out onto a terraced verandah.

"Bring your crown, and we'll go outside for a little while."

"Bring my crown? I . . . I really don't know exactly what to do with it," I mumbled. "I mean, it fits . . . uh . . . and it's beautiful. It just doesn't seem right to wear it."

Once again He gave me that broad, understanding smile. "You'll get used to it and figure out what to do with it."

I followed Him, carrying the silken box, still not sure what to do with it. We sat in the shade of a tree beside a clear, gurgling brook, and Jesus reached for the box. He thoughtfully removed the glittering crown and moved His chair closer to mine.

"Now," He began, "let's look at your crown."

I stared in wide-eyed wonder as He began to reminisce and explain every detail of my crown.

"You see this large amethyst? Do you remember the time you became very upset with Dan because he wanted to have the missionary couple over for dinner, and you were so weary of having company?"

I nodded dumbly in vague remembrance of the not-so-pleasant incident.

"But . . . but why that beautiful jewel when I was such a brat before they came?" I was quite confused.

"You invited them, didn't you? You cooked and prepared and cleaned up; and more than that, you listened to them. They were so frustrated and discouraged, and you helped Laura feel better about their situation. When they left, they felt that someone cared."

"But, Jesus, my attitude before they came was awful. I really didn't want them to come."

"But you *did* let them come, and you let yourself be used in spite of your weariness. Do you think that I always got excited about those throngs of people needing my attention?" He said with a twinkle in His eye.

I stared at the crown in silence. This was not what I was expecting.

Jesus continued, "Do you like this ruby? That's from the time during the Christmas rush when you stopped to visit with the clerk at Walmart about her sick husband."

I certainly did *not* remember that one. I had no idea what He was talking about.

"I like this pearl," He went on. "It came when you and Dan were planning to be missionaries in Argentina. Everyone was telling you how wonderful you were, but you knew in your heart that you really did not want to go at all.

"The more people praised your wonderful commitment and dedication, the more rotten and unworthy you felt on the inside. Do you remember how you had stopped praying, mainly because of your guilty conscience; and then the time when you finally dropped to your knees beside that blue bed and cried out, 'Dear God, *help!*' That was the sum total of your prayer. Do you remember?"

"Yes," I replied huskily. "But . . . I don't understand why . . . why this beautiful pearl? I was a mess!"

"Well," Jesus drawled slowly, "we preferred to think of you as a lump of clay.

"This emerald represents the time when Dan was sick, and you were so scared that he would never get well. You cried and cried in anger and fear and then just told Father that He was in charge because you gave up."

I certainly *did* remember that one.

"But, but . . . my faith was so weak. I was so frustrated that I didn't know what to do. I had reached the end of my rope."

"I know," He said softly. "It took a lot for you to realize who was in charge. You were a very strong lady, but you were never stronger than when you gave up and gave the whole problem to Father.

"Now," He continued with enthusiasm, "these beautiful sapphires are *very* special. They are from your parenting years. You were serving Me constantly during that time."

"Serving You? Constantly? I was so busy changing diapers and fixing meals and doing dishes and helping with homework and drying tears and . . . I hardly ever had a spiritual thought or did anything for the church. If I did remember to say a prayer at night, I usually fell into an exhausted sleep long before I ever got to the amen."

He chuckled gently, "Jenny, when you were investing every ounce of energy you had in those young lives, you were most definitely serving Me. I am all about children you know. I can't think of anything more important than little ones. I actually had to set my disciples straight on that issue a few times." He smiled with a faraway look as though recalling a special memory.

He looked down at the crown again. On and on He went, telling about incidents that I could not even remember when someone else had been helped, or times that I remembered as valleys when I had felt so weak and helpless that I had cried for help in utter brokenness.

Finally, I could not stand it any longer.

"But . . . but what about the time that I spent all those hours preparing and making the presentation at the Christian Teachers' Workshop? I felt really good about that. Or what about the time I had the dinner for the pastors and their wives? Or what about the time I organized the Ladies' Inspiration Day and spent all those hours making favors and chairing meetings, not to mention serving as hostess for the day?"

Now Jesus laughed gleefully. "Oh," He responded, "they're all on here too. See these teensy-tiny, little diamonds? But those were not your greatest moments. As a matter of fact, you probably got a lot of the glory for those at the time they were happening. Most of the time you were probably not even aware of the times when you were of greatest service and use to Father. But you can be assured that they never went unnoticed."

I was stunned. I stared at the crown—*my* crown—that represented the life I had offered so weakly to this wonderful Savior and Master. He knew me so much better than I knew myself. He loved me so much more than I could have imagined, as I was only now just beginning to discover. Just think, at my very worst moments, when I hated even myself, He was peeling through it all to find the seeds of goodness that He Himself had placed deep within my heart. I was awed by the moment of truth.

All at once this crown took on a whole new meaning. It not only represented my whole life with all its feeble attempts to serve this wonderful Master, but more than that, it represented His love for me through it all—a love that I could not even begin to comprehend earlier. This,

my crown, became a precious bond of love between us. I would treasure it always.

"Let's go back to the mirror and try it on," prompted Jesus. "Maybe it will seem more like yours now."

He lightly placed the crown in my hands and led me back inside to a full-length gold mirror in the corner of the room. I guardedly positioned the crown on my head. As before it seemed so light and fit so perfectly. But now it seemed more like my own, not because I had earned it, but because it was a gift, freely given to me from the deepest love of a caring Lord.

"Well now, Jenny. You are ready for your appointment."

For he has clothed me with

garments of salvation

and arrayed me in a

robe of his righteousness.

—Isaiah 61:10

God made him who had no sin

to be sin for us,

so that in him we might become

the righteousness of *God*.

—2 Corinthians 5:21

*W*ith no time but *now, appointment* seemed a rather contrived word. However, somewhere deep in the recesses of my mind, something about one appointment followed by something about judgment tickled my memory.

I had a very distinct feeling that something very important was about to take place. I looked up at Jesus with total trust. I knew from the crown incident that now, more than ever, I wanted to place myself in His hands. Still, a tiny seed of fear was struggling to emerge. I knew instinctively that whatever was about to happen depended on my Lord, who was also my Savior.

"Appointment?" I said weakly. "Are you going with me?"

"My dear little sister, I would never let you go alone. That's why I'm here. I've already taken care of all the preparations. Let's go."

He gently put His arm around me and guided me, still wearing my white robe and my crown, down the long hallway. We silently went up two more flights of stairs and entered an enormous hall covered with gold in every direction and brighter than the noonday sun.

At the end of the enormous hall were two colossal gold doors towering above me. I was numb with awe. At the touch of Jesus, the gold doors opened effortlessly.

With Jesus' arm still around me, I was ushered into an even more enormous room that blinded me with its light. For a little while I was being guided straight ahead by the gentle arm of Jesus around me, but I could not see a thing because of the brightness. Gradually, my eyes began to adjust to the dazzling light enough to watch my feet.

We stopped at the edge of what appeared to be a crystal-clear glass sea. I raised my eyes to behold a massive throne towering above me. There seemed to be a robe filling everywhere, although the face of the one sitting on the throne was not clear.

Suddenly I heard Jesus talking beside me, saying, "I have brought Jenny to see You, Father. She is a very

special servant of Yours, and I have so many wonderful things I want to say about her, although I'm sure You already know her quite well."

At that moment, I was feeling neither wonderful nor special. I was feeling *awful*. While Jesus was going on and on about certain things from my life—mainly more incidents that I didn't even remember—my mind was being bombarded with my own ugly sinfulness.

I was remembering other incidents—times when I had hated and criticized and lied and gossiped and times when I had been proud and uncaring and selfish and lazy. All those times I had been determined to have my way at all costs, no matter whom it hurt. All those times I had rationalized away what God wanted in order to make life easier or more pleasant. Many times. Ugly times. Endless times. They were all flooding back into my memory with precise clarity. This was all wrong. It should not be. It could not be. I began tugging on Jesus' sleeve. *"Jesus . . . Jesus!"* I whispered urgently, not caring that I was interrupting. This just could not continue. "Jesus, I must speak to You, now!"

Once again I was looking up into those unfathomably compassionate eyes. "I know, my child. Excuse us, Father, just one moment."

We walked slowly over to the edge of the glass sea separating us from the throne. I could not even raise my head as I began to speak. "Jesus, I'm sorry, but I cannot allow You to continue. It is wonderful, but it just will not work. I must remind You of the *real* me. There is a whole lot more to me than the part You are telling the Father about. I hardly know where to begin."

I was sobbing now, but this had to be said. I began relating the ugliest details of that part of me that Jesus seemed to be forgetting—the part that no one, *no one* but me, could know—the ugly, awful parts that lay deep within, well-disguised to most of the world.

As my shoulders heaved with uncontrolled emotion, I felt Jesus gently tilting my chin up to be able to look into my eyes. "Jenny, Jenny, I know. I know all of that. I know every detail about you, including the nastiest, dirtiest, most selfish thoughts you have ever entertained." He began telling me things about myself that no one, I repeat *no one*, could have ever known.

"How did you know?" I sobbed quietly.

"My dear, sweet child, I have known all these things for a very long, long time. You see, before you were even born, I took every detail of the things that you are telling me as a part of My life. On one horrible afternoon, I confessed them all to the Father as *My* sins.

"Jenny, you're right. Those were some awful times when you totally turned your back on Me. But that afternoon I recounted them all to the Father. Not only yours, but others. I confessed to murder and adultery and jealousy and fits of rage and lying and selfishness and pride and drunkenness—it all became a part of My life on that afternoon that I shall never forget.

"Jenny, our very own Father looked at My ugliness that afternoon and turned His back on Me. Because of those sins, We were separated. It was so dark and so lonely. But I took every one of those sins with Me into that darkness—darkness and separation that I endured for three long days. During those three days, I paid the awful price for them. It was my gift to you, and you accepted that gift from Me when you believed and surrendered your life to Me as a young woman.

"Your life is no secret, Jenny, but it has all been taken care of. You would not be standing here if you were anything but pure, because nothing impure is ever allowed to enter this place. Now, dry those tears and lift up that chin. You are about to see Father and receive His blessing. The account is settled."

As Jesus continued to look deeply into my eyes, I knew that He was seeing every detail of my most horrible ugliness, and yet there was no sign of recoiling, not even a flinch. Somehow when I looked up into those eyes that lovingly penetrated to the depths of my soul with nothing but total acceptance and approval, I had to believe—believe in my own worth and the purity that He himself had given me.

Maybe it takes standing before our awesome and holy Father to ever understand all those things that I had heard from my childhood, but finally, I could see them clearly, and it was wondrous. In an instant, while I stood in the shadow of Jesus as He continued His discourse about me, my mind was wiped clear. My past was gone. I

was standing before the Father wrapped in the dazzling white robe of *His* righteousness. The fog was clearing just as I heard the deep, gentle words coming from the throne, "Enter in, my child, my good and faithful servant."

My heart skipped an exhilarated beat, and I looked up to see that there was nothing separating me from the Father. He was beckoning me closer, and His face was looking into mine. Jesus quietly sat down next to the Father, a tender smile on His face.

I fell to my knees with unabashed adoration. Instantly I knew exactly what to do with my precious crown. I quietly removed it from my head and gently laid it at the foot of the throne where it belonged. I could only whisper, *"Holy, holy, holy, O Lord God Almighty. Only You are worthy to receive the glory of this crown."*

I do not know how long I spent in the presence of the Father. I remember worshiping with total abandon and the sounds of harps and angels singing and other glorious details that will always remind me of that first very private moment with Him.

These were all commended for their faith, yet none of them received what had been promised. God had planned something better for us so that only together with us would they be made perfect.

—Hebrews 11:39–40

Many will come from the east and the west, and will take their places at the feast with Abraham, Isaac and Jacob in the kingdom of heaven.

—Matthew 8:11

*F*inally, it seemed right to go. I turned around to find that Jesus was waiting to accompany me. As we reached the grand hall just beyond the throne room, the back doors suddenly burst open, and the hall was overrun with people. Each of them was wearing a distinctly different white robe. The first one I saw pushing through the back door was *my daddy*.

"Welcome, little girl!" he shouted as he threw his arms around me. My mother followed closely behind him, so happy to see her girl. She hugged me gently, softly whispering sweet words in my ear.

My brother, Rob, was right behind her waiting to hug his little sister. He pulled me quickly over to the side to meet Paul. Then he just had to introduce me to Peter. I should have known that my brother Rob would know everyone in heaven by the time he had been there a few minutes. Some things never change.

But the moment I had been waiting for came when a very handsome young man with freckles on his nose pushed through the crowd with that mischievous smile and twinkling eyes. "Hey, Grandma!" In that moment all eternity stopped for me as I touched him and hugged him and laughed with him again. Never again could he be ripped from my life. Never again would I feel the hole in my heart that could not be filled. Never again. We were together forever at home with Jesus. Wow!

Sometimes joy can only be fully appreciated when experienced through the prism of deep sorrow. Just for an instant a kaleidoscope of memories tumbled through my mind. I remembered the times sitting alone when I wanted to scream *no!* at the top of my lungs as reality crushed me once again—sweet Connor would never again be a part of my life. I remembered the waves of grief that would overwhelm me at unexpected moments when I saw a familiar picture or glimpsed a dark-haired boy from a distance. I remembered the awful pain of watching my precious son and daughter-in-law grieve from a place so deep and feeling completely powerless to help. I remembered the holidays and family pictures and birthdays and football championship games and graduations when Connor was so obviously missing and the silent pain that throbbed in my heart. I remembered sitting on the bench by his grave with the tears flowing freely, wondering what he would have looked like at this age. But now . . .

Everything I had believed was true—*more* than true. Joy simply exploded within me like the grand finale of a spectacular fireworks display.

We were all escorted into a gigantic banquet hall where we were served a feast in fine style. Rob arranged for me to be able to sit between my parents and Connor. Paul was on the other side of the table right in front of me. Wow! I finally got to ask Paul about his thorn in the flesh. He seemed to enjoy telling me all about it. He is still quite the theologian, and sometimes I still had a hard time following him.

Peter was exactly as I would have expected, and I loved him immediately. I saw Dorcas and Lydia visiting at the other end of the table.

Mary, Martha, and Lazarus sat right across from us. Martha was more relaxed than I thought she would be, but she was still busy telling Mary and Lazarus where to

sit and what to do. Mary seemed to be oblivious to it all, just enjoying everything that was going on around her. Mary and Martha both told me that they had been rooting for me, especially when I was having lots of company and working on my "hospitality attitude."

Mary, the mother of Jesus, was down the table a little way. She told me that she had especially cheered me on during those busy mothering years. She told me that she knew all about juggling several children at once, "Especially when one of them is rather independent," she said, casting a glance at Jesus with a twinkle in her eye.

Jesus, who was sitting at the head of the table, burst into laughter. "Now, Mom," He retorted cheerfully.

David, Moses, Noah, Ruth, John, Sarah, Abraham— everyone was there. It was wonderful! All in all, it was quite a celebration.

You may be wondering by now what we do up here all the time. I do not want to spoil any of the surprise for you, but I will say that there is never a dull moment.

We do have lots of parades. My dad still likes to recall the exciting parade when my mother arrived. He was so proud of her as he saw understanding and recognition begin to dawn on her face. He had introduced her to Anna and some of the other women who had been widows, and they enjoyed sharing stories. Anna had been rooting for mother during the years when she was alone after Daddy died.

The greatest time for me was when my husband, Dan, arrived. The tears were streaming down my cheeks as the limo rolled by. *(Happy tears are allowed.)* He quickly spotted me in the crowd, because I was the one cheering the loudest.

All of the kids and their mates are here now too. Imagine our joy as the limo pulled through the gate of pearl with the last one. Now we are all rooting together for the grandkids that are still running the race.

I do not know what is in store for me here, but all I can say is that so far the *first day* has been amazing!

Holy, holy, holy! All the saints adore Thee,
Casting down their golden crowns
around the crystal sea;
Cherubim and seraphim
falling down before Thee,
Who wast, and art,
and evermore shalt be.

~ ~ ~

When we've been there
ten thousand years,
Bright, shining as the sun,
We've no less days
to sing God's praise
Than when we've first begun.

Scripture References

Psalm 3:3
Isaiah 6:1–3
Isaiah 61:10
Daniel 12:13
Matthew 8:11
Matthew 16:27
Matthew 25:14–30
John 14:1–3
Romans 4:24–5:2
Romans 6:1–4
Romans 8:18
1 Corinthians 4:5
1 Corinthians 9:25
1 Corinthians 15:51–57
2 Corinthians 4:16–18
2 Corinthians 5:1–10
2 Corinthians 5:21
Ephesians 2:4–10
Philippians 3:14
Philippians 3:20–21

2 Timothy 4:7–8
Hebrews 2:5–15
Hebrews 4:9–10
Hebrews 7:22–28
Hebrews 9:24–28
Hebrews 10:35–36
Hebrews 11:39–40
Hebrews 12:1–3
James 1:12
1 Peter 5:4
Revelation 2:10
Revelation 3:5
Revelation 4
Revelation 5:11–12
Revelation 6:11
Revelation 7:9–17
Revelation 14:12–13
Revelation 19:11–12
Revelation 21–22:5
Revelation 22:12–14

About the Author

*B*eing the mother of six grown, married children and "Grandma" to twenty-six grandchildren, Rita Brown has devoted her life to her husband and family and to teaching others God's fundamental principles for daily living and for "getting your kids back to heaven."

Rita has experience in teaching women's classes, retreats, and seminars, and has served as a lecturer on the Oklahoma Christian Lectureship program. She enjoys writing Bible study material for in-depth group studies and is involved in encouraging and counseling young Christian wives and mothers. She has been a member of the Board of Trustees for Midland Christian School for twenty years, ten of which she served as president.

Rita loves being involved in the lives of her children and grandchildren. She spends much of her time attending

football, basketball, volleyball, and baseball games along with a few track meets and golf tournaments. Keeping up with birthdays is one of her greatest life challenges, and of course Christmas is always quite a production.

Having served as missionaries in Brazil during their early years of marriage, Rita and her husband, Dale, continue to travel extensively, often observing mission areas and encouraging missionary families. Brazil holds a special place in their hearts, as well as more recently Uganda, where they were able to travel for the adoption of their newest grandson, Moses. Both are also involved with various organizations that promote conservative family values. Dale serves on various Christian boards, including the Board of Regents of Pepperdine University.

At this writing, Rita and Dale have celebrated fifty-one years of marriage and are spending as much time as they can with their first great-grandchild. At home in Midland, Texas, they are members of the Golf Course Road Church of Christ where Dale served as an elder for sixteen years.